DISCOVER
The Iroquois

by Margaret McNamara

Table of Contents

Introduction

The Iroquois are Native Americans.

confederacy

longhouses

nations

Native Americans

reservations

the Iroquois

See the Glossary on page 22.

3

Where Are the Iroquois?

Some Iroquois are in Canada.

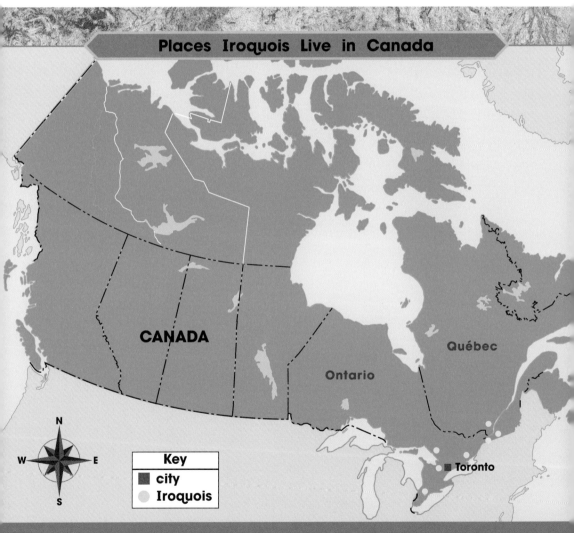

Places Iroquois Live in Canada

CANADA

Québec

Ontario

Toronto

N
W   E
S

Key	
■	city
●	Iroquois

▲ Some Iroquois live in Canada.

Some Iroquois are in the United States.

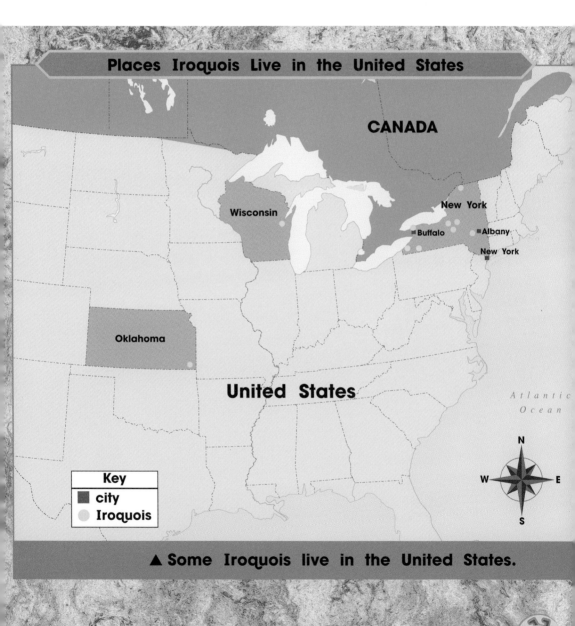

Places Iroquois Live in the United States

CANADA

Wisconsin

New York

Buffalo

Albany

New York

Oklahoma

United States

Atlantic Ocean

Key
city
Iroquois

N
W E
S

▲ Some Iroquois live in the United States.

Some Iroquois are on **reservations**.

▲ Some Iroquois live on reservations.

Some Iroquois are in cities.

▲ Some Iroquois live in cities.

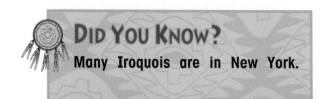

DID YOU KNOW?

Many Iroquois are in New York.

How Did the Iroquois Live Long Ago?

The Iroquois were hunters long ago.

▲ The men were hunters.

The Iroquois were farmers long ago.

▲ The women were farmers.

Iroquois were in forests long ago.

▲ Iroquois were in forests.

Iroquois were in villages long ago.

▲ Iroquois were in villages.

Iroquois were in **longhouses** long ago.

▲ Iroquois were in longhouses.

Iroquois were in **nations** long ago.

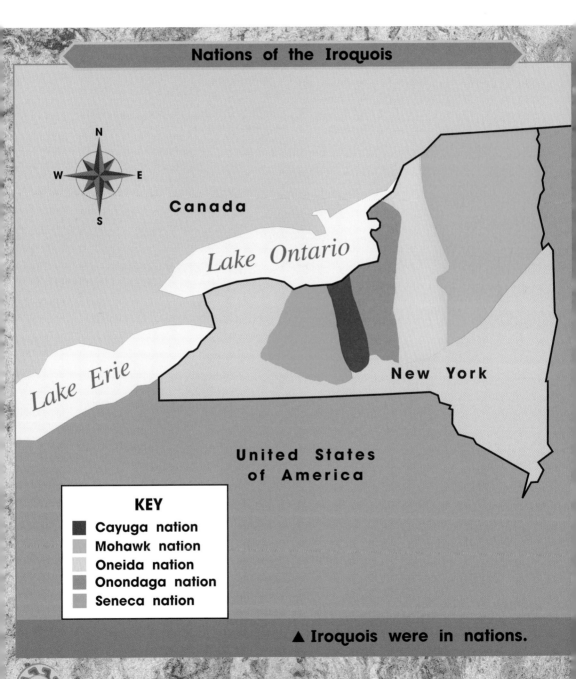

Nations of the Iroquois

Canada

Lake Ontario

Lake Erie

New York

United States
of America

KEY
- Cayuga nation
- Mohawk nation
- Oneida nation
- Onondaga nation
- Seneca nation

▲ Iroquois were in nations.

Iroquois were in a **confederacy** long ago.

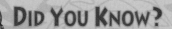 ▲ Iroquois were in a confederacy.

DID YOU KNOW?

Another nation was in the confederacy.
This nation was Native Americans.
This nation was not Iroquois.

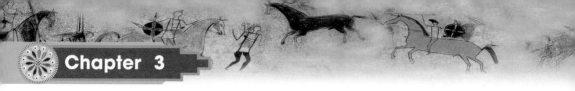
How Do the Iroquois Live Now?

Iroquois have nations now.

▲ Iroquois have nations.

Iroquois have a confederacy now.

▲ Iroquois have a confederacy.

Iroquois have many different jobs now.

▲ Iroquois have different jobs.

Iroquois have special art now.

▲ **Iroquois have special art.**

Conclusion

The Iroquois are Native Americans. Some Iroquois are in Canada. Some Iroquois are in the United States.

▲ Iroquois are Native Americans.

How Do the Iroquois Live Now?

have nations
have a confederacy
have many different jobs
have special art

Glossary

confederacy the nations of the Iroquois

*Iroquois were in a **confederacy** long ago.*

longhouses homes of the Iroquois

*Iroquois were in **longhouses** long ago.*

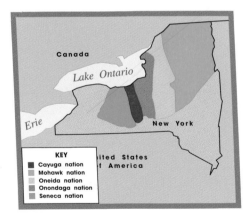

Canada

Lake Ontario

Erie

New York

KEY
- Cayuga nation
- Mohawk nation
- Oneida nation
- Onondaga nation
- Seneca nation

ited States
f America

nations groups of Iroquois

*Iroquois were in **nations** long ago.*

Native Americans the first people in North America

*The Iroquois are **Native Americans**.*

reservations land where Native Americans live

*Iroquois are on **reservations**.*

the Iroquois Native Americans

The Iroquois were hunters long ago.

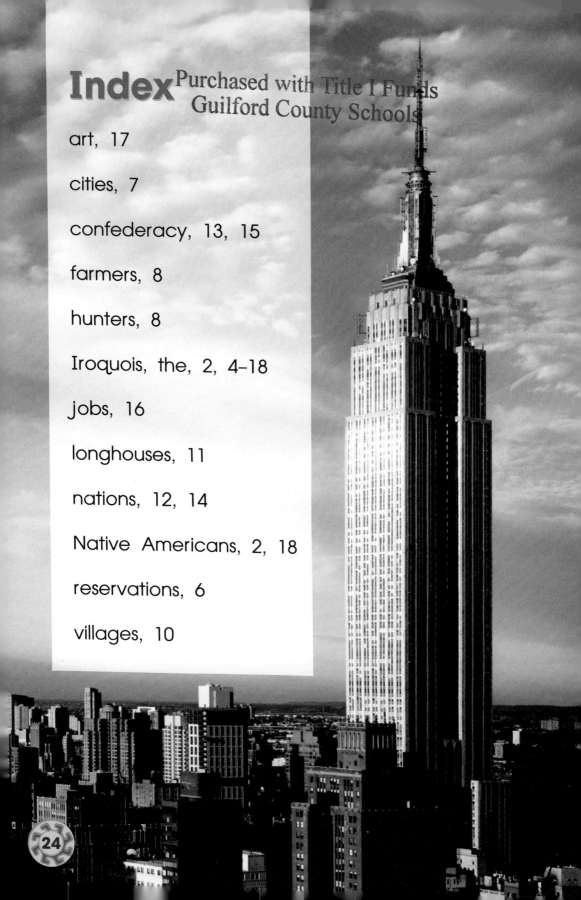

Index